MY BROTHER MiCHAEL HAS AUTiSM. HE iS 11 YEARS OLD AND I AM 6 YEARS OLD.

SOMETIMES IT FEELS LIKE I AM THE OLDER SISTER.

BECAUSE MY BROTHER HAS AUTISM IT IS HARD FOR HIM TO SPEAK.

I DO THINGS THAT MICHAEL SHOULD
HAVE LEARNED BECAUSE HE IS OLDER.

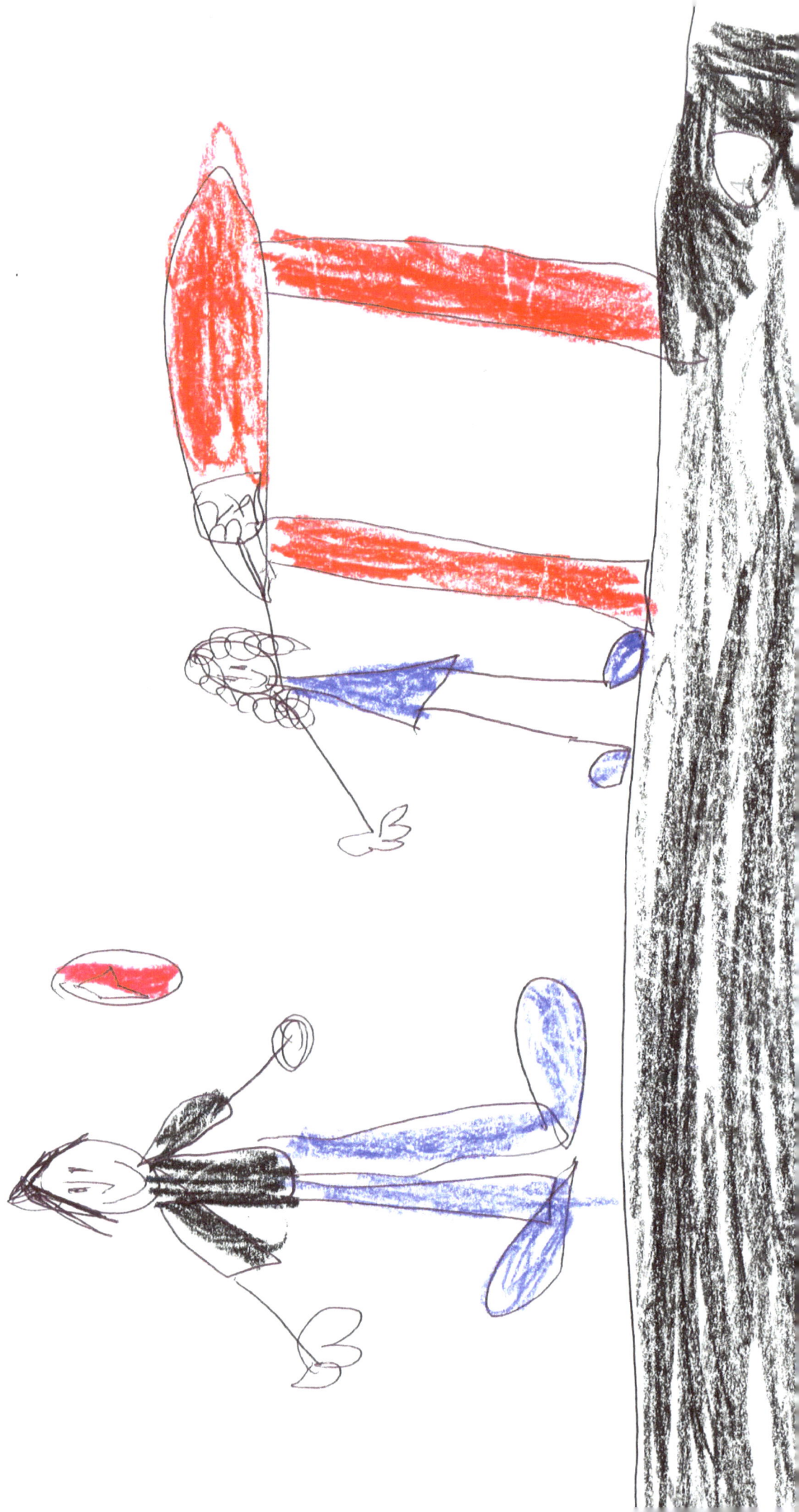

WHEN SOMEONE ASKS ME ABOUT AUTISM, I TELL THEM ABOUT THINGS HE DOES SO THEY CAN LEARN ABOUT AUTISM.

MICHAEL BANGS ON WALLS AND BOUNCES
ON HIS BIG BALL

MICHAEL LOVES TO PLAY WITH HIS TOY
SNAKE THAT TWIRLS IN THE AIR.

MICHAEL LIKES TO SPIN A LOT AND I LIKE TO DO THAT WITH HIM.

HE NEVER GETS DIZZY.

I TEACH HIM STUFF I KNOW LIKE I AM
HIS TEACHER

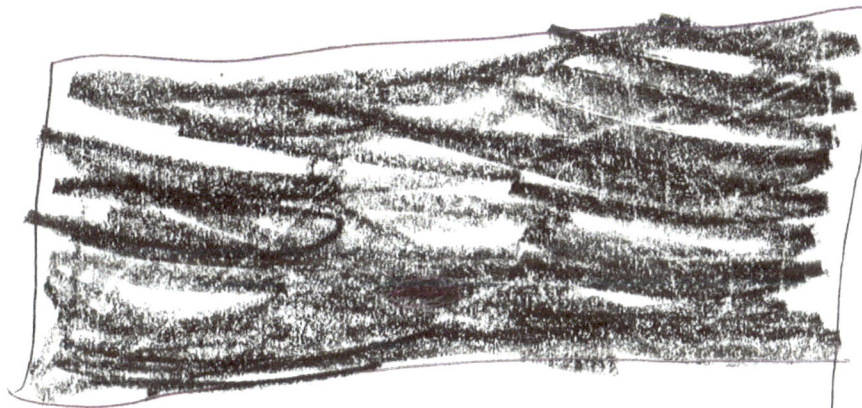

MICHAEL HAS THERAPISTS THAT COME TO
OUR HOUSE AND THEY DO PUZZLES WITH
HIM AND WORK WITH HIM.

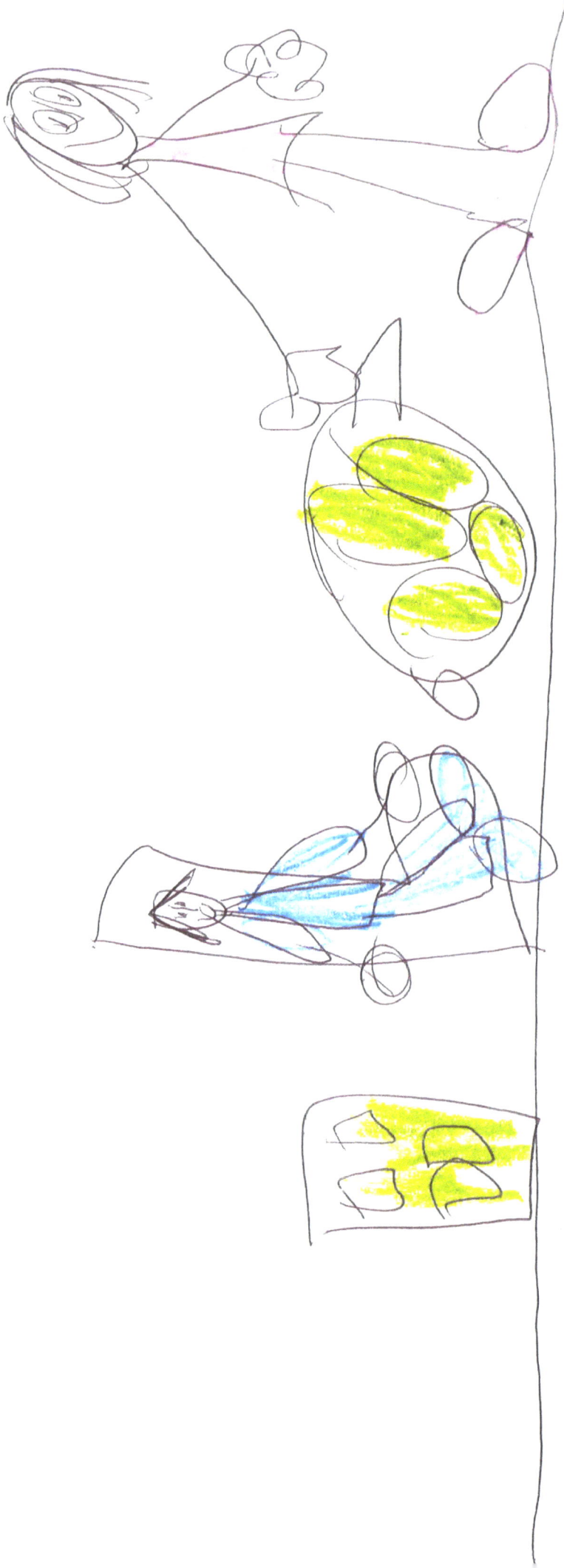

SOMETiMES THEY TAKE BREAKS AND
TAKE A WALK WiTH HiM.

I SOMETIMES GO ON WALKS WITH THEM
OR I LIKE TO PLAY WITH HIS THERAPY
STUFF

SOMETIMES MICHAEL'S THERAPISTS MEET WITH MY MOMMY AND DADDY AND HAVE A MEETING.

I SIT AT THE TABLE AND LISTEN TO HEAR WHAT THEY SAY ABOUT MICHAEL.

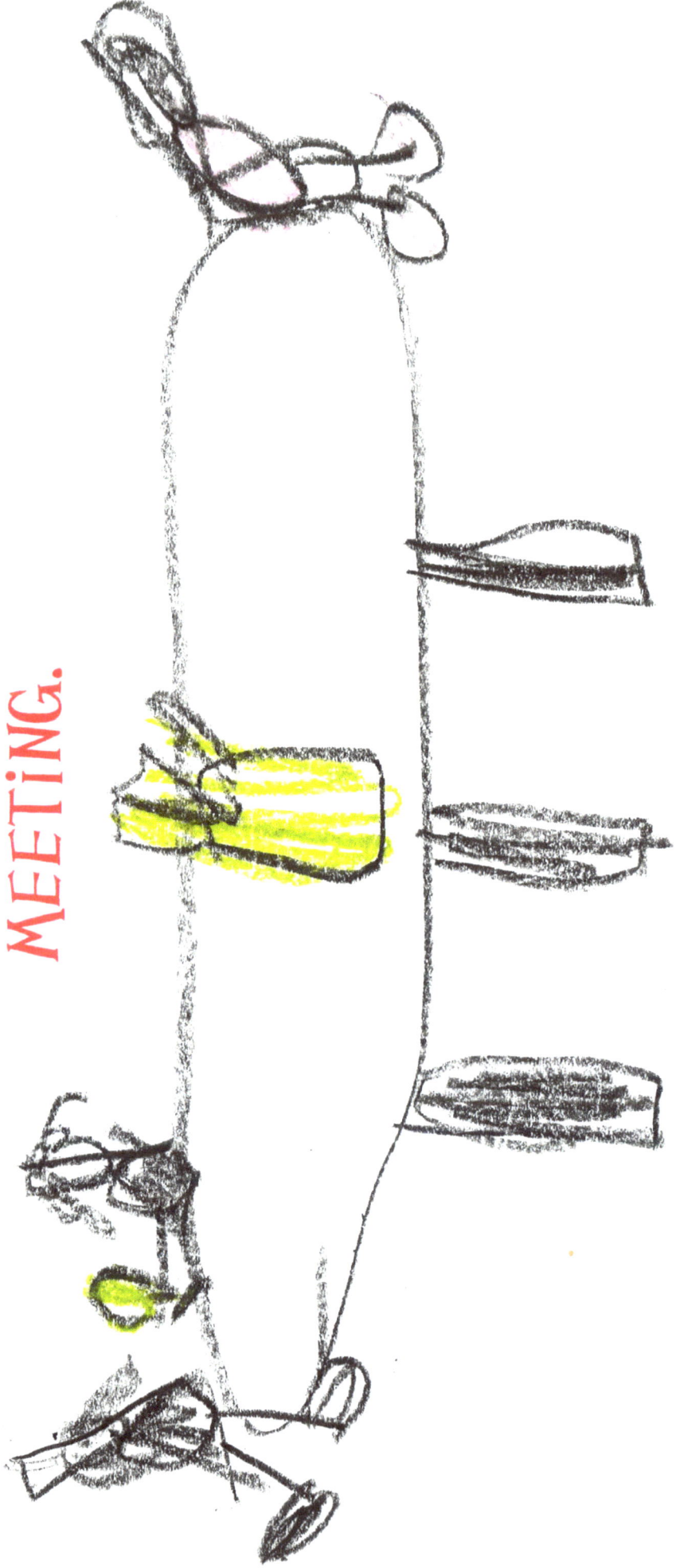

SOMETIMES WHEN I TELL MY FRIENDS MY BROTHER IS AUTISTIC THEY THINK I AM SAYING MY BROTHER IS "ARTISTIC".

MY FRIEND ASKED ME HOW DOES MY BROTHER LEARN STUFF AND WHAT DOES HE DO AT SCHOOL?

I SAY HE LEARNS HIS A,B,C'S AND NUMBERS.

SOMETIMES MY FRIENDS ARE AFRAID OF
MICHAEL AND THINK HE MIGHT HURT THEM.

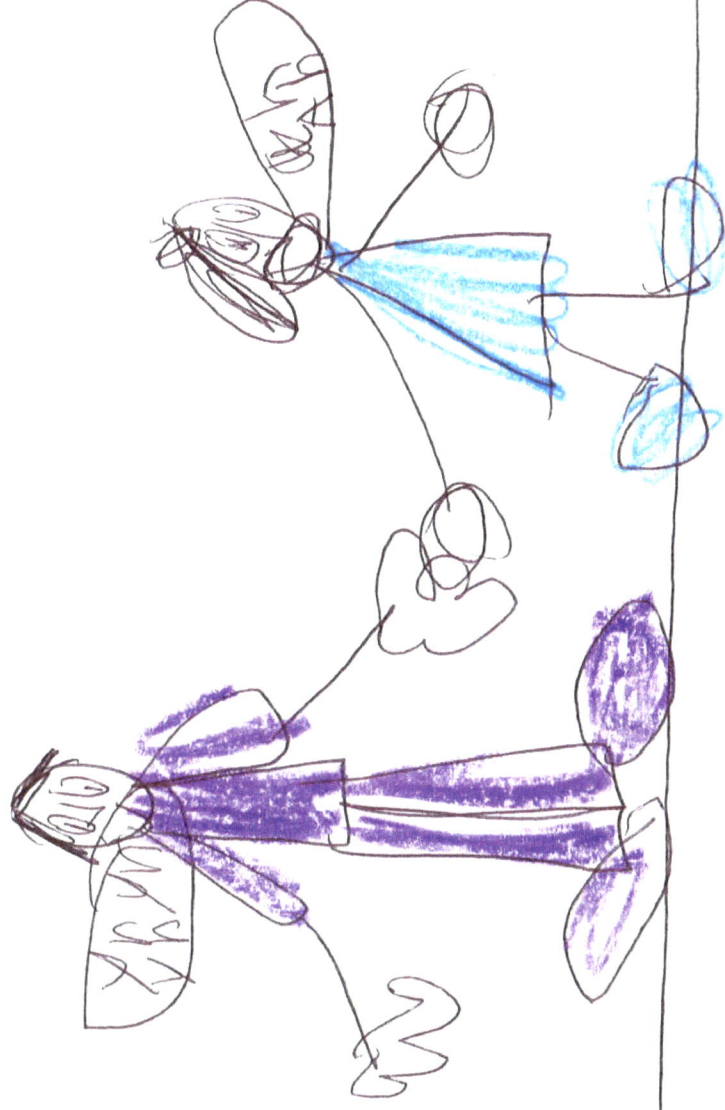

I SHOW THEM THAT HE WILL NOT HURT THEM
AND THAT HE IS NICE TO ME ALL THE TIME.

SOMETIMES IT IS EASY AND SOMETIMES
IT IS HARD TO HAVE AN AUTISTIC
BROTHER

MY FAVORITE THING TO DO WITH MICHAEL
iS GO OUTSIDE iN OUR BACKYARD.

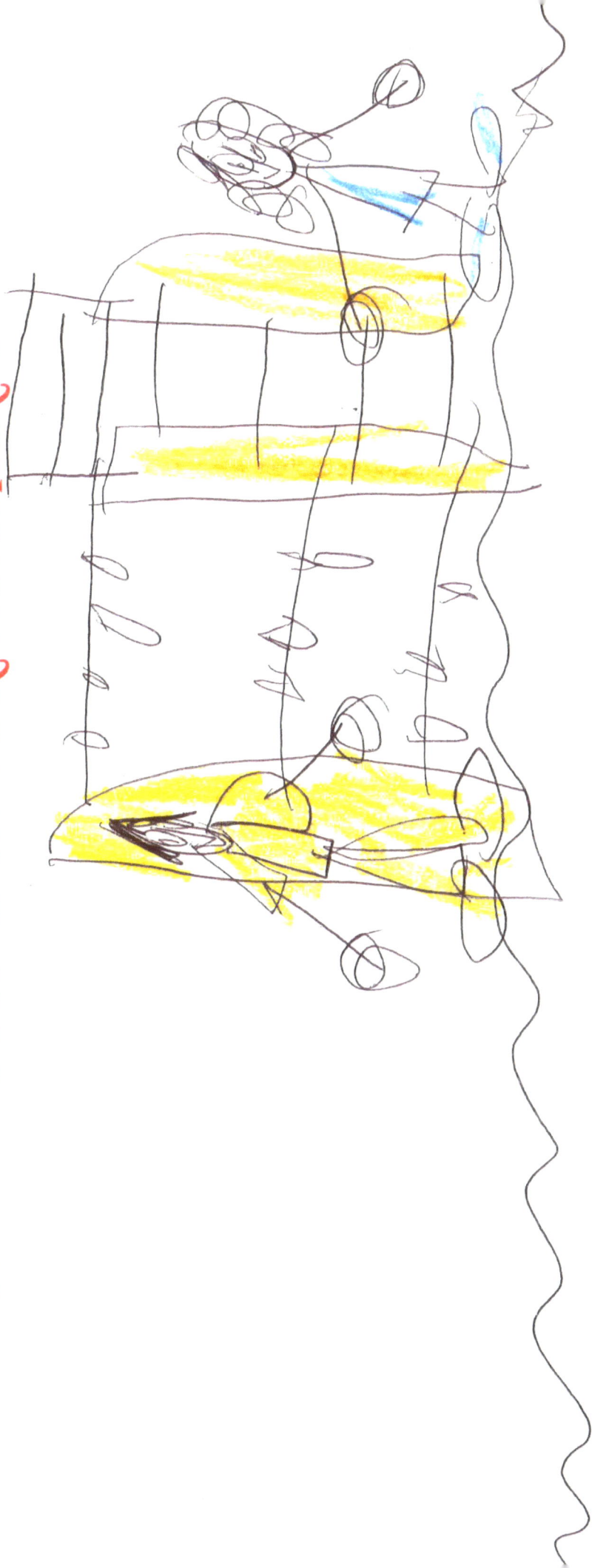

THAT iS BECAUSE WE BOTH LiKE TO PLAY
OUTSiDE.

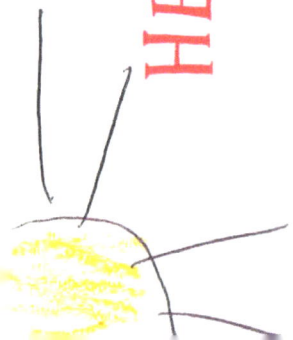

HE ALWAYS GOES ON THE RED SWING AND
I GO ON THE BLUE SWING.

IF I GO ON THE RED SWING MICHAEL WILL
NOT GO ON THE SWINGS AT ALL.

I LIKE TO GIVE MICHAEL HUGS AND
KISSES AND HE LIKES IT TOO

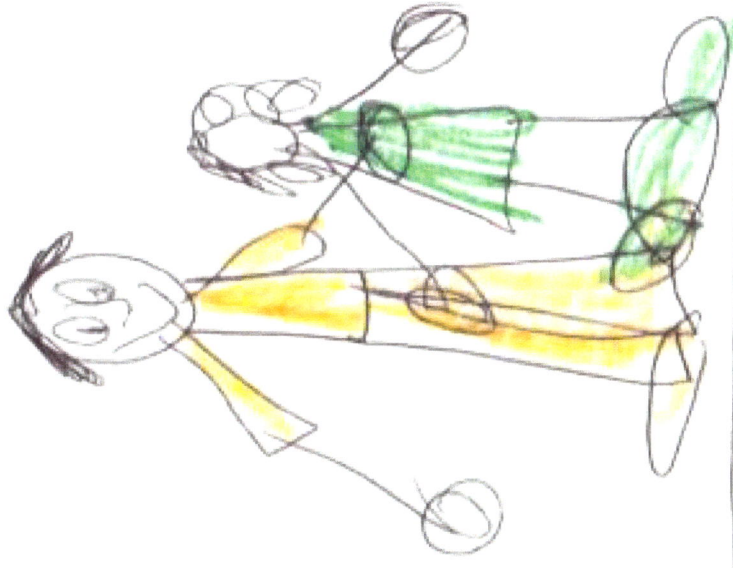

I LIKE TO DO THE ITSY BITSY SPIDER
SONG WITH MICHAEL

IN THE CAR I READ MICHAEL BOOKS, PLAY PATTY CAKE, AND WE LOOK OUT THE WINDOW TO SEE STUFF

I TALK TO MiCHAEL AND SOMETiMES I DO
SiGN LANGUAGE SO HE CAN UNDERSTAND
WHAT I SAY

IF I DO NOT UNDERSTAND HIM, HE USES HIS BOOK THAT HAS PICTURES IN IT SO HE CAN POINT AND SHOW ME WHAT HE WANTS

AT DiSNEYWORLD, WE SAT iN THE FRONT SEATS AT SHOWS AND WENT TO THE START OF LONG LiNES BECAUSE MiCHAEL WAS AUTiSTiC.

THAT WAS COOL.

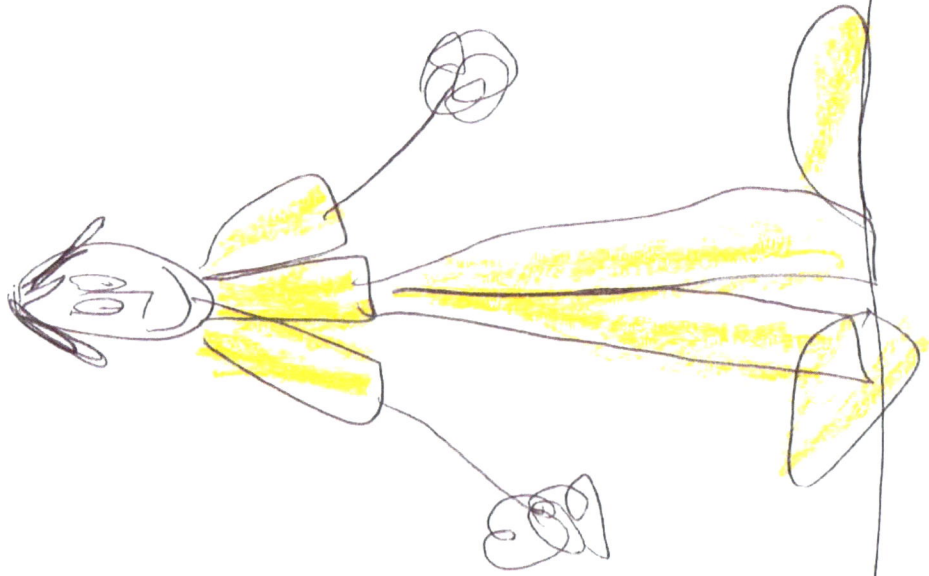

MICHAEL IS SWEET AND KIND AND WILL
ALWAYS STAY THAT WAY.

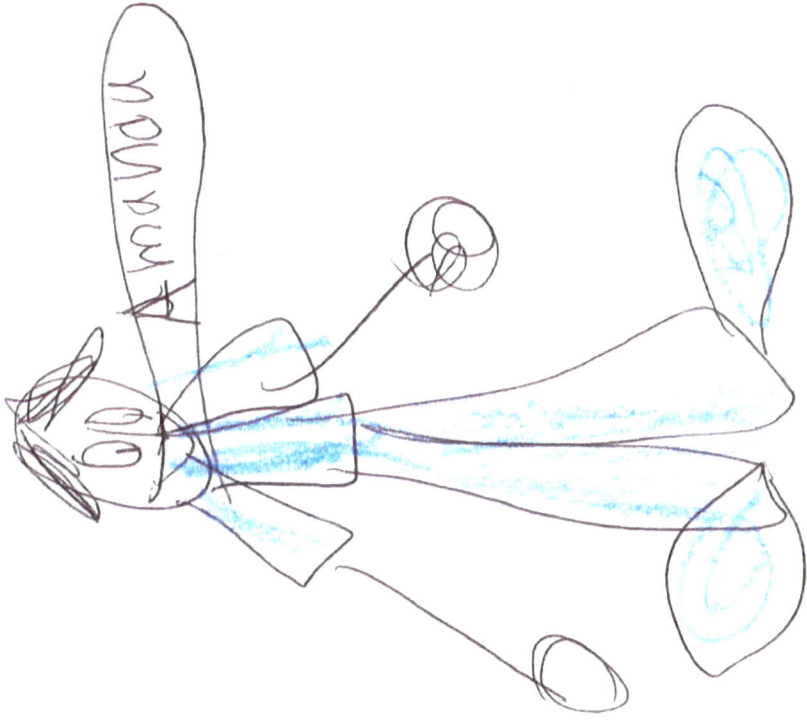

WHEN MICHAEL GETS OLDER, I HOPE HE
CAN TALK SO HE CAN LEARN STUFF AND
TALK TO ME, MOMMY, AND DADDY

www.ingramcontent.com/pod-product-compliance
Lightning Source LLC
Chambersburg PA
CBHW060900270326
41935CB00003B/49